Twenty Restaurants
Valencia, Sp
A Guide to Eating Tap..., Paellas, Wine,
Ham and Understanding Menus

Marc Luxen

Preface

I went to live in Valencia to write a Dutch and a Dutch-Indonesian cookbook, and have eaten at many places here while I have been doing that (the books are nearly finished). I live in El Carmen, the old town, and I decided to write this short book about eating in El Carmen, and the peculiarities of eating in Spain. A specialised little book like this can do a much better job than bigger guides. Twenty local restaurants that my friends and I like. Simple workmen's places with nice locations, and all right, places where they serve modern food, and classic places, one mentioned in the Michelin guide, a nice mix. We are talking about the 10 to 20 euro restaurants here.

First, I will tell you something about the peculiarities of eating in Spain. The Siesta system, the "paella system", all about ham, wine and other important drinks, and the *menu del dia*. Then I will give you a list of common dishes you can use when deciphering a menu or what a waiter is trying to tell you. Following is a list of restaurants where you can go and experience good food. With phone numbers, opening times, a clear map, a link to Google maps so you can use your smartphone to find these places easily, and a short description of what to expect. In the print version there is also QR code as well as link to Google Maps, so you can scan with your mobile directly to Google maps. Last, a list of Spanish food terms.

I used my own preferences in choosing the restaurants. I like simple, classic cooking. Not creative but correct. Most trendy or fusion cooking is not for me. Drinking out of empty jam jars while eating prawns in chocolate-sauce with Thai *nam pla* with a "*Carpaccio*" of mushrooms on the side is not my thing. Another thing I care about is that the menu changes regularly, or at least some of the dishes. A restaurant serving the same menu year in, year out, disregarding seasonal influences has lost interest, and bored, uninspired cooks who just go through the motions in the kitchen. Finally, a restaurant should do only a few things. A jack of all trades is a master of none, and nowhere is that more true than in a restaurant.

Spain is at the frontier of modern cooking. But you do not need me to find those restaurants: the Michelin guide does that well than anyone else. In fact, because one and two star restaurants are much cheaper here than in Northern Europe, you should visit one if you are into your food, certainly. For instance, one Michelin star Restaurant Riff of Bernd Knoller , close the main railway station, does a fantastic lunch menu of Spanish food for 35 euro, with an optional wine pairing for 16 euro extra, a true bargain if you ask me: http://www.restaurante-riff.com/

You can visit the Facebook page of this book at fb.me/eatinginvalencia

Contents

Introduction

The siesta system means that the earliest you can have lunch is at two pm. Well, some restaurants will serve you at half past one, but that is it. Now, when you walk hungry into a restaurant at two, the waiter will be slightly annoyed, because you are a bit early. You will just have to accept it. If you want to eat what the Spanish eat, you will have to eat when they eat. Oh, by the way, if you think this is a late lunch, prepare for a shock for dinner. The Spanish close shop at eight or even nine a clock, and eat dinner (or tapas) after work of course. So, it is perfectly normal to go to dinner at ten. Nine is a bit early, and eight is possible, but again, you will be the first in an empty restaurant. Yes, this is madness, but you are not going to reform a whole country on your holiday, so just accept it.

Most restaurants offer a lunch menu. This is for many people the main meal of the day. At night, they often have tapas. No Valenciano will ever, ever eat paella at night. So I advise you to follow this custom. Enjoy a lunch menu, and have your tapas at night. Yes, I know you would rather have it the other way around, but live with it. In fact, many of the simple nice restaurants will close after lunch. So, when you see a menu you like on your stroll around, and say to each other: "let's go there tonight" be sure to check if it is in fact open for dinner, and if so, mentally prepare to wait until nine. I will mainly be talking about the lunch menu here, but I will you tell you if the restaurant is open at night. Oh, and to tell you straight away: a **Tapa** is a small portion, a **Ración** is a big portion.

Your ideas about Spanish cooking may not be the same as how they think about cooking here. Let's take paella (and by the way, you do NOT pronounce that like "pa-yellar" but as pa-ay-ya. Just put the "Y" sound one syllable more at the back). Anyway, when you and me think about paella, we think about rice and seafood, maybe chicken and of course lots of that delicious chorizo, right? That is how the Ramsay's and the Jamie's do it on the telly, and tell you to do in their books. Wrong. And very wrong too. If you really, really want to piss off a Valencian waiter, send your paella back because there is no chorizo in it. No, just joking, do not do that, please. It is really dangerous, and you will give the rest of us a bad name, and we have a dubious reputation already. So be prepared that things are a bit different?

Another thing you need to be prepared for is the noise the Spanish make in simple restaurants and on terraces. No whispering, far from it. They shout, stand up, anything that goes with a good time. It is always a nice experiment to start talking loudly, well screaming, to your table companion in a restaurant. In the Northern Europe, the whole room would fall silent and be disturbed looking at you. In Valencia, no one bats an eye. Too busy making noise and having a good time themselves.

The menu is usually outside, written on a blackboard or so. That might make things easier sometimes, but not necessarily, because many things will be not available, substituted with other things, and there will be most likely additions too, the specials, – and these are the fresh things you really want to order. In addition, in Valencia they have the annoying habit to use their dialect (which they want you to call a language) instead of Spanish. Don't worry, they are quite similar. It is really not that unusual to walk into a restaurant and have the waiter ask you: ¿que quiere? ¿What do you want? Of course, you have no idea, so the correct answer is: ¿que hay? ¿What do you have? (Don't forget the inverted question mark). Now, you are likely to be the first customer with your non-Spanish daily rhythm when you are starving at two o'clock, so he doesn't know either. He will now either shout to the kitchen to find out what he is serving today, or he has it written down on his note pad. He or she will now read your options in high speed machinegun-like Spanish, so you maybe pick up a few familiar words, and cling to those like a drowning man clings to small pieces of driftwood....... *Ternera*? *Gazpacho*? Something with *pescado*?

So let's find a way out of this. If the menu is posted outside, decipher it BEFORE you go in. Decide what you want, remember how that sounds in Spanish and order it. If that doesn't work, just take the waiter outside and point at the menu. This is the most elegant solution for all parties, I think. But be sure to try to understand the specials. You can ask for the menu (saying "menu" or rather "*carta*" and looking confused should do the trick). You might be allowed to have a look at their notebook, where they wrote down the menu of that day for themselves, because written Spanish is easier to understand than spoken Spanish. Do not worry, it is all part of the fun. Spanish waiters may seem brusque and blunt, but they usually are quite friendly and genuinely want to help you. They will take their time too. *Tranquilo, hombre.*

But the best trick is to know what to expect. Let this book help you. The number of dishes is fairly limited really, because a Valencian cook likes to use ingredients that are local, and food is steeped in tradition here. Let's first talk paella, because you will not be able to escape this in Valencia.

Paella and other rice dishes

For most of us, a paella is about what is in it, but to a Valenciano, it is about the rice itself, mainly. Rice is the heart of Valencian cuisine. You really should not underestimate this: rice in the kitchen of Valencia is just as important as say in Chinese cuisine. Over 120.000.000 kilos of rice (6000 big tanker trucks) are produced every year, on the rice paddies just south of the city in a region called La Albufera (which is , by the way, worth a visit when you have time). The most highly valued is Bomba rice. It is perfect to cook paella or risotto-style rice, because it is "sticky and pearly": it has a high starch content, and it does not break or split when you cook it, but just expands. You can buy it in small cloth bags on the Central Market, it is a nice thing to take home with you, or to give as present. **So, the first thing to get into your head is: rice dishes in Valencia are about the rice, not what is in it.** (Actually, the first thing is: Valencian rice dishes have no chorizo in them).

A true paella is made to order, and because of this, you need to order it for at least two people, and you will share a pan (paella means pan, it has the same root). A good paella has a delicious crust at the bottom: the *socarrat*. It is one of the reasons why they use a big flat pan to make paella, and the rice should never by more than say, two fingers deep at most. Be sure to eat all of it, it is the best part of the dish! Note that the prices will be per person, and expect to pay at least around 12 euro for a made-to-order paella.

If paella is part of a lunch menu, it is not made to order, but the cook made an enormous pan of paella before opening. It is usually prominently placed to entice potential customers. They will also sell portions of paella for take-away. This type of paella is much cheaper, and, unlike made-to-order paella, they will serve it to one person only. There will be no crust, and it will be cold or tepid. Expect to pay around five euro per portion.

And remember: paella is a lunch dish, never for dinner!

Some say Paella should be made on a wood fire (you will see the word **leña,** wood Spanish**)**, and it is true, it adds a certain smokiness to the rice. You will find it hard to find a paella made on a wood fire in the centre of Valencia, I haven't found one yet. You need to go to the coast to get the real thing. Two restaurants near the sea far outside the city centre are the places to go if you really want to take your paella seriously. Casa Carmina and Nouraco are two good options. They are outside the scope of this book, but I will give you the links. Combine a visit to these restaurants with an excursion on the lakes and rice paddies, there are organised tours like these: http://www.visitalbufera.com/

http://casacarmina.es/

http://nouraco.com/en/

However, there is no such thing as "Paella" on a Valencian menu. There are types of paella, and some things that you probably would see as paella, or a mix of paella and risotto, are not even called paella. So, here comes the first handy list:

Paella Valenciana: served in a flat pan, with chicken (**pollo**) and rabbit (**conejo**), and vegetables (**verduras**) that are in season, but often runner beans or white beans. Sometimes, snails (**caracoles**) in their shells are added too: if you find that scary, leave them at home and just don't eat them.

Paella de marisco: The same, but with seafood (**Mariscos**): almost always mussels, squid and shrimp, unpeeled.

Arròs (arroz) del senyoret:. This is paella de marisco, with the seafood taken out of the shells (it means prepared for a lord"). It is one of those paella's that you are not allowed to call a paella. To me a paella, by any other name, would still taste like paella.

Arròs negre (arroz negro): Another seafood paella (de mariscos), but this time the rice has been made black with the ink of the squid in it. The ink makes the rice taste a bit more "fishy", but it is mainly a visual thing, I think.

Paella de verduras: Ah, we are allowed to call a Paella a Paella again! Made with vegetables (verduras). This is really seasonal, and it can be anything from green beans to artichokes. This is not a strictly vegetarian option, because the broth will be chicken broth or something other not vegetarian.

Fideua: All these dishes are also made with Fideua, a sort of short spaghetti, the kind that you would use in soup. They are just as popular as the rice varieties. I guess it makes a change if you get too much rice, but I personally find these dishes very inferior to the original rice dishes, and so do most of my non-Spanish friends. My Spanish friends are divided on the subject. Try it if you have some more meals to go, but if your time is limited, stick to rice.

Arros (arroz) a banda: This is not a Valencian dish, but comes from the Alicante region. However, they sometimes are broad-minded enough in Valencia to still serve it. It is rice cooked in a fish stock and saffron, with little or nothing added to it. So: plain rice boiled in fish stock. Mostly served with the ubiquitous garlic mayonnaise called *aioli*.

The next dishes are more soup or risotto style, and they can be delicious, truly delicious, even if, like me, you are not a big fan of rice. They are served in a deeper pan, usually made of ceramics.

Arros (arroz) meloso: (Literally "sweet rice", because the texture reminds them of honey – I did not make this up, I swear. It is not sweet, by the way). This is the most risotto-like dish (but without butter or cheese!). It is usually made with seafood (Mariscos), but chicken, rabbit, vegetables are possible as well. Always made to order.

Arroz meloso con bogavante: This is an absolute winner in Valencia. This is arroz meloso with local lobster and other seafood. If you do not go for paella, this is the one to try.

Arroz caldoso: This is a much thinner meloso, it is really almost rice soup. Again, seafood, chicken, it is all possible.

Arroz al horno: Rice baked in an oven. It is much nicer than it sounds really. A nice crust on top, and it usually filled with chickpeas (**garbanzos**), pork ribs (**costillas de cerdo**), blood sausage (**murcilla**) and vegetables (**verduras**), but everything goes.

Ham (Jamón) and sausages (Embutidos)

Ham is a religion in Spain. On the central market you can get ham of around 200 euro per kilo, and that is not in a super expensive exclusive stall. It is worth to try a few slices, so you can say to yourself you ate the best and most expensive ham of your life. It will cost you around five euro for this experience, a bargain I think.

Ham is either **Serrano** or **Ibérico**. Serrano is normal raw ham, you probably know it. It is not what you came here for, it is an industrial, bio-industry product. Ibérico is what you want: this ham is the pride and joy of Spain. It is made from the Ibérico pig, an indigenous pig to Spain and Portugal. There are four grades of Jamón Ibérico, categorised by what the pigs get to eat and how long the hams are cured. Lower grade hams are cured around a year, high grade hams up to three (**reserva**) to four (**gran reserva**) years. The best is **Jamón ibérico de bellota.** *Bellota* means acorn. Iberian piglets eat cereals and acorns until they are nearly one year, all free range. Then it becomes even better: the last three months spent out in the *montanera*, roaming the forest for acorns. They need to eat 7 kilos of acorns per day to reach the magical 160 kg to need to get the jamón ibérico de bellota demonination. These acorns are so important because they come from the holly oak and they are rich in oleic acid, the same acid that gives the taste to olives. This gets into the fat of the animal, and into your ham, which melts like olive oil in your mouth. **Jamón ibérico de recebo:** the Ibérico pigs eat diet of cereals and acorns and the hams are aged for at least three years, but they do not roam the last months of their lives. **Jamón ibérico cebo de campo** is made from free range Ibérico pigs but they only get cereals, no acorns. Finally, **Jamón ibérico de cebo** is a ham made from Ibérico pigs but industrial.

Sausages are made from the rest of the meat: **Chorizo (de cerdo) ibérico:** a chorizo, and **Lomo (de cerdo) ibérico:** a cured pork tenderloin of the pig. Ibérico pigs. **Pata Negra,** which means "Black hoof is another name for the Ibérico pig.

It goes further, because the Spanish also have names for places where the meat is on the ham. I don't expect you to be really taking this in, but please indulge me: **La Maza** is the backside of the leg largest and best part of the ham and tastiest. **La Babilla** or **Contramaza is** the less fatty, narrower muscle at the front of the leg". **La Caña** is the part closest to the hoof. It is quite tough, and they usually cut it cubes to serve with a drink. **El Codillo** is located between the hoof and the main bulk of the ham. It is the toughest part of the ham. **La Punta** is the part right at the tip of the main bulk of the ham and it is fatty and tasty too.

Wine, vermouth and cocktails

Ever since several studies in the Journal of Wine Economics proved that experts do no better than novices in tasting wine, I regard the wine world mainly as a marketing circus. Google "wine tasting junk science", read and free yourself.

Of course, when a waiter knows the wines they are selling and the dishes, I would take their advice. Decent wine is shockingly cheap in Valencia (which is a problem in itself!), around three euro for a bottle in a shop can buy you a very nice wine indeed. The house wine, **vino de la casa,** is always drinkable, always a simple, easy wine. Sometimes, when you order a glass of wine: **"una copa de vino",** they will ask you to choose between a Valenciano and a Rioja. You are in Valencia, the choice is obvious. In most cases, well almost always, they will not go through the ritual of tasting and approving your wine in the common restaurant. What a relief! Red wine is sometimes served from the fridge, this is normal. In fact, when the wine is not that good, it masks the rough taste. Loads of wines your drink in Valencia actually come from Requena Utiel to the west. **Moscatel** is a fortified white desert wine, you will sometimes get a glass for free. **Roble** means it aged on wood, and the wine has that smoky oaky vanilla taste. **Reservas** and **Gran Reservas** are always oaked-aged. I prefer a cleaner, lighter taste, but up to you of course.

Cava, the Spanish Champaign or Prosecco is excellent and a bargain. At the supermarket Mas y Mas they sell bottles of chilled cava for less than then three euro, and it is delicious. It is sometimes drunk at the beginning of the meal, but mostly at the end.

Aqua de Valencia ("Valencian water") is a deceptively strong mix of orange juice, cava, vodka and gin, with some sugar.

Sangría does need a description. I never see many locals drink it, but it can be delicious and refreshing, and much stronger than you would expect, usually

Vermut (vermouth) is white (**blanco**), rose (**rosado**) or red (**rojo**, not tinto for some reason). It is a very common drink in Valencia, and does not have the old-fashioned feeling it has in Northern Europe. It is served in a big glass with ice cubes, an olive on a pick and a slice of orange in it. Very often is it is home-made (**casero**)

How to enjoy the lunch menu (menu del dia)

A typical **menu del dia** gives you the choice between a number of starters and mains, with a desert and/or coffee. There usuallyis no real difference usually between starters and mains, and many restaurants just give you a list of what there is, and you can choose two. There usually is the option to choose only one, but the price will be not much less, so I never do that. You will have weird choices between say a salad, a plate of pasta, or paella, followed by another pasta or paella, or grilled fish. Anything goes, it up to you to balance your meal how you like it. In some restaurants you will get a few starters to share, this is on the menu as **centro de mesa** (on the middle of the table) or **a compartir** (to share). You will nearly always get bread (**pan**), because this is seen as the staple food at any meal, much like people from Northern Europe regard potatoes as an invariable part of a meal.(A potato in any form is regarded as a vegetable here). You can always have as much bread as you like. It says on the menu *pan incluido*: including bread. A drink is also nearly always included, and you can chose wine, beer or soft drinks. So "drink and bread included" looks on the menu like: *bebida y pan incluido*. In fact it is so normal that they usually tell you explicitly when the drink is not included: *bebida NO incluido*.

Note: On a Saturday, the *menu del dia* is usually a bit more expensive, and in many restaurants, there is a special menu (read: paella) on Sundays

For some obscure reason, there is never any pepper on the table, and if you ask for it, it has to be hunted down from the most obscure corners of the restaurant. You just have to accept that (or do like me and bring your own). The two things you do get are salt and olive oil, but these are the very things you will not need. Food in Valencia is nearly always salty and oily enough, often way too much to my liking. Again, you just have to accept that. Salads are never dressed. Sometimes you get a salad to share included in the menu (this is not necessarily advertised), and sometimes it is a dish you can chose. They are simple affairs of lettuce, tomato and onion rings, with an olive or two. There was a time where I also carried mustard to make a proper dressing live at the table, Meat steaks are always a bit disappointing to me, because they are cut way too thinly, and as a consequence, are always well-done (or beyond that point even). I find the way the Spanish ruin their steaks hard to forgive, when I see them slice wafer-thin slices of delicious red tuna or entrecote on the market. Meat just gets olive oil and salt, fish might get olive oil and parsley, which is surprisingly nice, especially with lemon, which you will always get with fish or chicken. In the off-chance they ask you how you would like your steak, it goes like this:

Cocida? (The cooking?) Or, Como le/les gustaría la carne?

Very Rare –Muy poco hecha

Rare –Poco hecha

Medium rare Al punto

Medium –*Regular*

Well Done –*Muy hecha*

(There are other terms too, but these are easy to use and understand for you and the waiter)

If you order wine, a few things can happen. If you order wine in the cheaper restaurants, where the workers have lunch, they might simply put a bottle on your table, full or half full. In these restaurants people see wine almost as food, and the will not drink more than a glass or so with their meal, and feel no need to finish the bottle. So you get it next of it is not empty, easy. Don't make the mistake to complain you didn't order a bottle, but only a glass. The waiter won't understand, and if he does, they will simply say: "well, take only one glass then if that is what you want". You can drink the bottle if you like, and they rarely charge you extra for that. On the other hand, when you order a bottle of wine while the drinks were included, you might pay for the whole bottle and forego your drinks. It doesn't really matter, because the wine will be around five euro a bottle anyway. A nice solution is to order a bottle of wine and two sparkling water, so everything is clear. Don't worry too much about it, you are on a holiday, drink wine and pay the man the few euros.

Water is never included, but often, you can order a big bottle of mineral water for one or two euro. Normal water is called **aqua sin gas** (water without gas), and sparkling water **Aqua con gas** (you get it). Sparkling water is always served in a small bottle, but normal water may be in a big bottle. Just say "**aqua sin gas grande**" and make a big sign with your hands, they will understand.

Let's talk desert: *postre*. More often than not, these are not written down on the menu. Sometimes you get desert AND coffee: **postre Y café** and sometimes desert OR coffee **postre O café**. In case it is OR coffee, you can have coffee after desert but you will have to pay for it. Speaking of coffee: you will have to decide beforehand how much milk you want in it. None at all is a **café solo**, a little bit is a **café cortado** (a "cut") coffee, and a lot is a **café con leche.**

You had your meal, and now the waiter asks something like: "¿posrocafe?": You want a desert or coffee? You will get a list of desert and you don't understand anything of it, but do not worry. There are things that are always there. They are included in the common dishes list underneath, but there is always, always **Flan** (thick custard with caramel), and sometimes **Torta (de queso, de manzana)** cheese cake, apple pie). Look at the list to find out what they are. Here we go:

Common dishes

A la romana - Battered and deep fried

Albondigas - Meatballs, in tomato sauce and peas

Atun plancha - Grilled thin slice of tuna

Bacalao al horno/plancha - Cod from the oven (**horno**, or **forn**) or from the grill (**Plancha**).

Bistec de Ternera - This is a thin slice of beef, do not expect a steak. It is grilled, and served with salt and olive oil. Invariably served with fries or baked potatoes. Ask for some Aioli, and you have a nice dish.

Boquerones - Small sardines. As a tapa they are usually filleted and pickled, as a dish lightly battered and fried heads still on. You can eat them whole, or leave only the heads

Caldo - Broth, but usually with meatballs, or one big meatball and vegetables

Canalones (de carne) - Cannelloni with minced meat

Chipirones - Small squid, usually breaded (**rebozadas**) and fried.

Cocido - Soup or stew with chickpeas vegetables, potatoes and meat

Conejo asado - Grilled Rabbit

Crema catalana - Runny cream custard (I never noticed any difference with **Natillas**)

Crema de Calabaza - Pumpkin cream soup

Crema de puerros - Soup of creamed leek

Embutidos - Cold cuts of sausages

Emperador Plancha - A thin slice of grilled swordfish

Ensalada russa - Russian salad, served with breadsticks

Ensalada tomates atun - Tomato salad with tinned tuna

Ensalada Valenciana - Salad lettuce, onions, and tomato

Entremeses - Cold cuts

Esgarrat - Strips of roasted bell peppers and strips of salted cod.

Flan (de huevo, de café, de chocolate) - A custard dessert with runny soft caramel: plain (huevo), coffee, or chocolate

Fresas con nata - Strawberries and cream

Fruta - Fresh fruits usually Orange (**naranja**), Apple (**manzana**) or Strawberries (**fresas**), pine apple (**piña**), peach (**melacotón**), melon (**melón**) or watermelon (**sandía**)

Gazpacho - Cold tomato soup with, cucumber, bell pepper, onion and garlic.

Gazpacho monchego - Not gazpacho at all, not even a soup! Pieces of pasta, (flatbread actually) mixed with a quail, pigeon, hare or rabbit stew.

Habas con Jamón - Broad beans with bacon

Horchata (orxata) - The traditional drink of Valencia, made with a kind of almonds, to be precise: tiger nuts. It tastes like earthy almond milk. You have it with **fartones**: light fluffy sugared pastry fingers.

Lenguado - Fried sole with lemon

Lomo de (anything) - A filet of anything

Magro - A cut of pork, and served as a stew with tomato

Mejillones al vapor - Mussels, usually boiled with some pepper corns, and not much else

Merluza plancha - Grilled hake with you guessed it, fried potatoes and lemon

Montadito (or Pincho) - A slice of baguette with something nice on it, kept together with a small skewer. Anything goes.

Morcilla - Black pudding, blood sausage with rice and garlic, creamy and delicious

Natillas - Runny cream custard (I never noticed any difference with Crema catalana)

Papas bravas - Fried crispy potatoes with garlic mayonnaise and a spicy sauce

Pechuga de pollo empanada/plancha - Chicken breast (**pechuga**) pounded flat and grilled (**Plancha**) or in a light batter deep fried (**empanada**). Served with lemon and potatoes

Pescaditas (a la romana) - Battered deep fried whole small fish

Pez (pescado) Espalda - Skewered cubes of fish, grilled

Pincho (or montadito) - A slice of baguette with something nice on it, kept together with a small skewer. Anything goes, even croquettes.

Pollo asado - Grilled chicken

Pulpo (or pulpitos) - Octopus (baby octopus). Usually boiled and sliced thinly, pulpitos served whole

Puntillas Rebozadas - Small pieces of deep fried lightly breaded squid

Rape - Monkfish. Order this when you can. It is either grilled or from the oven in a tomato sauce

Revuelto - Scrambled egg, not revolting. Not eaten for breakfast. Usually with cooked ham (**jamón York**) or mushrooms (**setas**)

Salmoreja - A sort of gazpacho, but smoother and garnished with raw ham and hard-boiled eggs (to me, it is the same as gazpacho, really)

San Jacobo - A rolled up schnitzel, chicken or pork, filled with ham and cheese, breaded, and deep fried.

Sardinas plancha - Grilled sardines, well more fried sardines. Usually lightly floured

Secreto - A tender cut of pork, usually grilled, Secreto Ibérico is from the Ibérico pig.

Sepia plancha - Grilled cuttlefish

Sopa del dia - Soup of the day

Sopa de lentillas - Lentil soup

Tallarines (salteados) - (Fried) Noodles

Verduras Salteados -, Crema de- - Fried vegetable, cream of vegetables

Recommended restaurants

These are the restaurants that I like, and my friends like. If I don't mention a restaurant here, it does not mean it is bad, not at all, it can be quite good. I have decided not to make a list of bad restaurants, because restaurants change owners, I have my own tastes and opinions, and I did not want to write that kind of book. I know you want to eat outside, but most good restaurants are inside only. The Spanish are absolutely allergic to sun, except on the beach. They complain about sun and heat like we complain about rain and cold. The first ray of sunshine in spring, and you hear everywhere *¡que calor!* "it is so hot! I like to sit outside too, so most restaurants I mention have a terrace. I will tell you if there is a terrace or not.

You can find the address, a telephone number if they take reservations, opening hours, a map, and a link to Google maps for use on your smartphone and a short description. If there is no telephone number you cannot reserve there. I present them in alphabetical order.

I tried to cut the map so you would always see a familiar landmark on them, for easy orientation. This is mostly the Plaza de la Reina, the Central Market or Plaza de Virgin. A slight complication is that street signs are sometimes in Valencian and sometimes in Spanish, with no system. They look alike though, so use common sense: Carrer Cavallers is Calle Caballero, it is not hard. However, one important landmark has two very different names, though: the central square La Plaza de la Virgen in Spanish is Plaça de la Mare de Déu in Valencian (Virgin square and Mother of God square).

All maps: © OpenStreetMap contributors: http://www.openstreetmap.org/.

Blanqueries

963 91 22 39 Tu-Sat 13:30 to 16:30 and 20:30 to 11:30, Sun lunch only
http://restauranteblanqueries.com/

This restaurant is a bit different, it is more classic French style inside.
(recommended Michelin). Spacious, light with perfect service, fresh food, well
prepared, modern, and beautifully presented. The menu is 20 euro, including a
drink, but the wine list is so good and so affordable The menu includes three
starters per person, and main and desert to choose. Reserve for Friday, Saturday
and Sunday. Worth it, in my opinion, but if you want to outside al fresco tapas
experience, this is not what you are looking for.

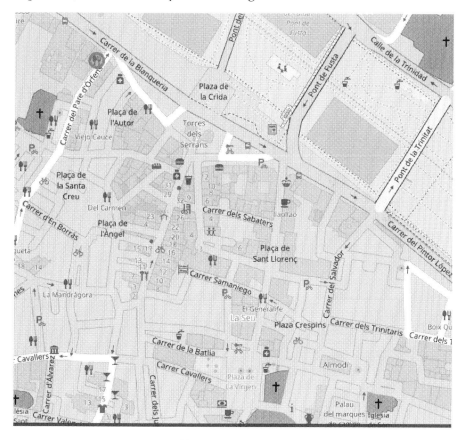

© OpenStreetMap contributors https://goo.gl/maps/JdaFs6SKNWG2

Boatella
Plaça del Mercat, 34 Tu-Sun 08.00 01.00

The tapas are good, the prices maybe a little high, but still very reasonable, the service is friendly, and the location is smack-bang right in front of the Central Market: it does not get any better. The terrace is great, and there is an enormous choice of traditional tapas. True, you will find not only locals, no way around that on a location like this, but it is so enjoyable here. Up to you.

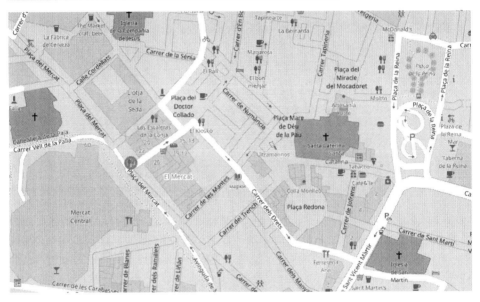

© OpenStreetMap contributors https://goo.gl/maps/7YowgTxmy9w

El Bon Mejar

Zurradores, 8 Sat-Sat 13.00 17.00

Next to the Pony Pisador. Absolutely dirt-cheap no-frills Spanish *menu del dia*, with tables outside. No cars, a quiet alley on a small square, and quick and friendly service. A working people's lunch place: 9 euro for the menu, including wine.

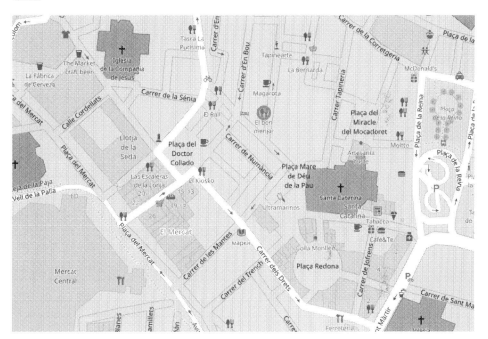

© OpenStreetMap contributors

https://goo.gl/maps/idPjqM7Bkxv

El Generalife
Carrer de Navellos, 11, Open every day, 08.00 to 12.00

There are two restaurants close to another restaurant called "Generalife", so pay attention! This is cheap restaurant, more a bar. Don't order the paella. But, with a view of the Cathedral and the square, with a pint for less than two euro, and a menu of grilled fish, salad, chips, desert and a glass of wine for 7,50 euro, you cannot complain. The deserts are home-made, and surprisingly good.

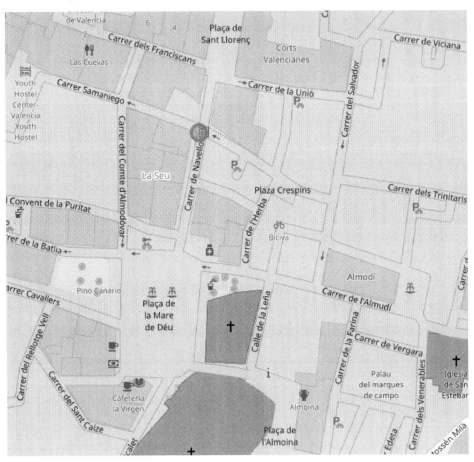

© OpenStreetMap contributors

https://goo.gl/maps/vsPhP5K7Xw82

21

El Kiosko

Carrer dels Drets, 38

Closed on Monday as far as I could find out.

A simple tapas/ **menu del dia** restaurant on the lovely square Placa del Doctor Collado, very close to the central market. It has a nice terrace, but the inside is your typical Spanish interior, no frills, tables and chairs. Menu is around 12 euro, lunch only, tapas all day and night. The location is great, the food normal Spanish, without any pretentions. Popular with locals.

© OpenStreetMap contributors

https://goo.gl/maps/r4kLNVNuJc12

El Molinon
Carrer de la Bosseria, 40 Every day 13.00-1600 and 20.00 00.00

A wide range of fresh, nice dishes, Asturias-style, so something different. It is a Sideria, so try the Cider, I would say. You can have three dishes and a drink and desert for 11 euro, so when you don't go alone, you have your table full of different dishes, all delicious (not on Sundays). Unfortunately no terrace, and a bit dark, but it is a great experience of Spanish food.

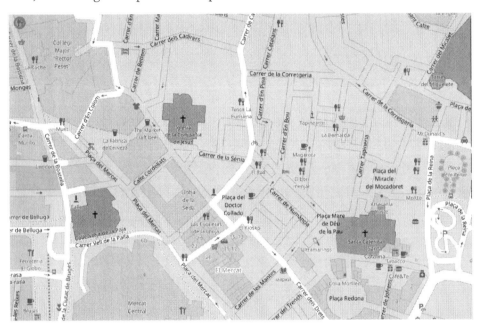

https://goo.gl/maps/FWR2dCipTuT2

El Pony Pisador

963 92 14 43 calle zurradores 7 Wed-Sun 12.00-00.00,Mon-Tue 19.30-00.00

https://www.facebook.com/ElPonyPisadorValencia/

The fancier neighbour of the El Bon Menjar. More creative, but still traditional. Menu 15 euro, no wine. If you want to try the **Arroz meloso con bogavante,** the "risotto style" paella with shrimp and lobster, this is a good place to do it. You will have to pay extra on bit on top of the menu price, but it is worth it. Start off with a *vermut rojo casero*, a home-made red vermouth.

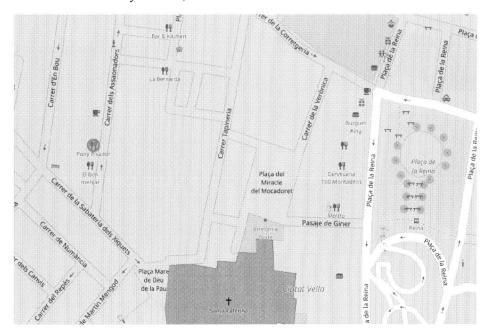

© OpenStreetMap contributors

https://goo.gl/maps/gXTYaR7rAYs

El Rall

963 92 20 90 Calle Tundidores 2 Daily 11:30-16.00 and 19.00–00.00

http://www.elrall.es/

Nicely located restaurant, on a tiny square that they made into a terrace. They specialise in paella's made to order, and the Jamón (raw ham) outside on placeholders, where they cut the thin slices by hand is a nice touch. It has a small sea town, cosy feel. Not very popular with locals, but the location is nice and the food is fine, and it is a nice place to enjoy a paella for two, for around 14 euro per person, drink not included.

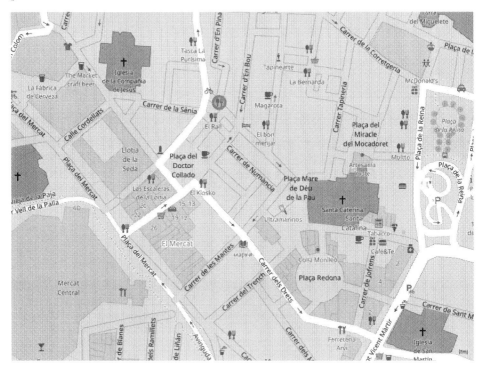

© OpenStreetMap contributors

https://goo.gl/maps/iHMYpb6ApUR2

La Comisaria
96391079 Plaza Arbol 5 Mo-Sat 20.00-00.00, Fri –Sat13.30-16.00 and 20.00-00.00

http://lacomisaria.com/

Well, I have to confess, this is a fusion cuisine as far as I can stand, but, I like it here. Modern dishes, creatively prepared, for very reasonable prices. Menu 12 euro, drinks not included. You can see the chef preparing dishes, and for a while they even had a projection of the kitchen on the wall opposite the terrace, so everyone could see what was happening. That is gone now, unfortunately. If you are into modern-ish food, give it a go.

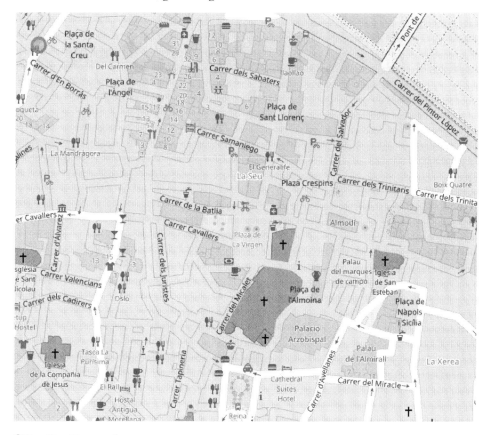

© OpenStreetMap contributors

https://goo.gl/maps/dqQdCp1DgZr

La Coqueta

960 91 45 41 Calle Baja 42 Tu-Sat 19:30 – 01.00

https://www.facebook.com/lacoqueta.restobar/

A quaint little restaurant around the corner from where I live, with modern, creative fresh food. It is dark, with no terrace, but hey, this the old town! A meal with wine will set you back around 15-20 euro, and be sure to ask for recommendations on the wine, because they have a very good **bodega**!

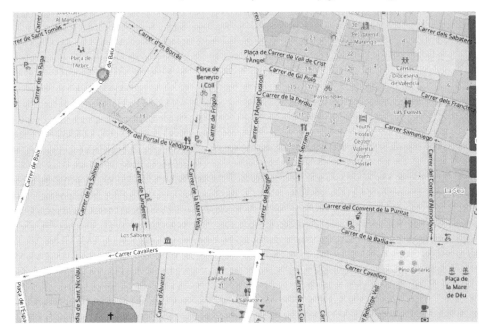

© OpenStreetMap contributors

https://goo.gl/maps/MzbxfzXr6hL2

La Pitusa

963 91 12 19 Carrer del Pare d'Orfens 4, Daily 11.30-00.30 pm, Sunday Paella

http://lapitusarestaurante.es/

The best location for a terrace on Placa El Carme, near the fountain. Simple food, a touch different from classical Spanish, but not much. Menu around 9 euro, drink not included. Lovely place to sit.

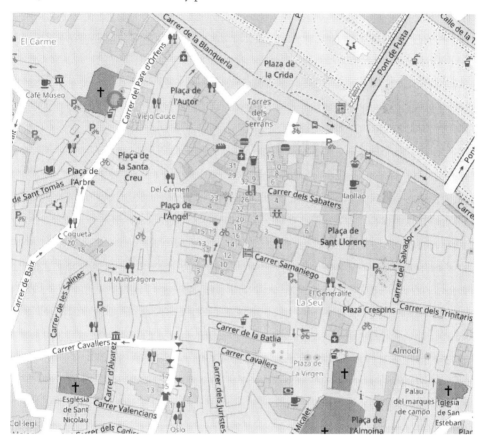

© OpenStreetMap contributors

https://goo.gl/maps/wEiQknRzpo22

La Taverna d'Enric

960 62 68 33 Carrer de la Corona, 7 wed-sun lunch and dinner, Sunday lunch

https://www.facebook.com/profile.php?id=100011742908460

Simple Spanish food perfectly done, for very reasonable prices. The service is friendly and very quick. I wish there was a terrace, or that the nice interior was not ruined by cheap energy saving light bulbs. The perfect place for a wonderful quick lunch.

© OpenStreetMap contributors

https://goo.gl/maps/Ww7c2cV8hLR2

Lizarran
Plaça de l'Ajuntament, 8 Daily 08.30 -23.30

http://lizarran.es/

I have doubted a long time if I wanted this restaurant here, because it is not a restaurant, but a bar, and because Lizarran is chain all over Spain. It is just outside El Carmen. But I like it, because I have never seen anywhere else so many different Tapas and Montatidos on such long bars. You order a drink, take a plate, and chose from at least 40 different options, all good and fresh, though not perfect: after all, it is a chain. Afterwards, they count the skewers on your plate, and you pay, about a euro per tapa. Hey, it is cool this-is-Spain experience, so give it a go.

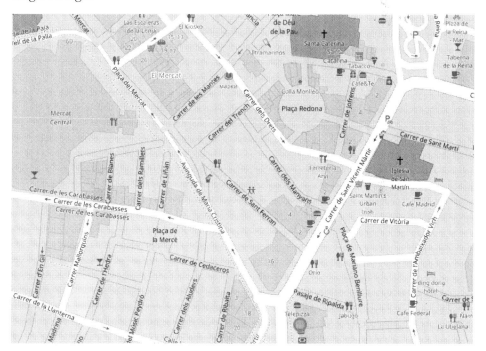

© OpenStreetMap contributors

https://goo.gl/maps/s9HFgdkBCJU2

Los Sabores

963 92 62 17 Carrer de Landerer, 1, Weekdays 07.00 until 17.00

It looks awful from the outside, but inside there is a nice dining room and a lovely quiet garden, and it is just steps away from the Cathedral and the square. The food is nothing special but very adequate and fresh, and for 10 euro, including drink, and this fantastic location, you cannot complain.

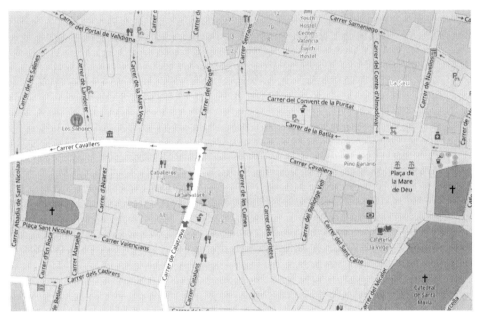

© OpenStreetMap contributors

https://goo.gl/maps/7QjCByzwqPs

Mercat Central, Central Market

This is not a restaurant, but it is too good not say a few words about it, because there are many things to eat here, and to take home. I suppose you come in through the main entrance. You enter a square place, with a separate wing on the right for the fish. In the middle is a round central place with a big tower on top. The butchers are situated in the outside circle, the sellers of ham more to the left. The fish stalls have their own wing to the right. Interspersed are vegetables stalls, pickled goods stalls, poultry vendors, cheese stalls and anything you can think off. Many of the ham and cheese sellers sell sandwiches, or a platter of cold cuts, sometimes with a glass of wine. Just walk around, and you will see people eating and drinking. At the back, to the left, is the tapas bar of Michelin chef Ricard Camarena. In the fish department, there are vendors that will open oysters to eat. Freshly squeezed fruit juices are everywhere.

To take home: Bomba rice, the rice for paella. Pickled garlic, which must be one of the great pleasures of life. Capers in salt, not pickled. Put them 6 hours in water before use, and you have the natural taste of capers. Olives, of any, and I mean, any type. Saffron, readily for sale because it is necessary for making paella. Take some of the special paprika they use to make chorizo (buy the "Murcia" variety) Of course, Jamon Ibérico, vacuum sealed. Chorizo sausages. Also, give the smoked tuna/bonito a chance: serve them thinly sliced with olive oil.

That should do the trick!

Muez
960 06 78 22

Plaça del Mercat, 20, Every day except Tud 09.00 -22.00, Fri Sat until 00.00

http://muez.es/

This is a small eco-friendly local produce restaurant with simple, very nice dishes, mostly vegetarian. It has a nice terrace, and it doubles as a bookshop. The location is perfect, and even more so ever since cars were banned from that street recently. Central, healthy, and quiet, what more can you want?

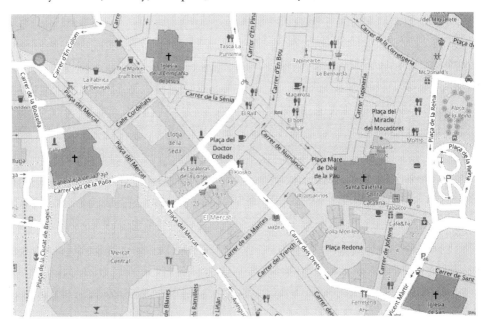

https://goo.gl/maps/LUPYF9MY4sz

Osteria el carme

Mercado Municipal de Mossén Sorell, Mon-Sat 11.00 - 15.00, Thu Friday also 17.00 - 20.30

Situated in the glass market on Mossén Sorell, this is a very simple stall where they sell delicious oysters per piece and preserved fish like smoked tuna, anchovies in oil. An oyster and a glass of Cava cost around five euro.

https://laostreriadelcarmen.com/

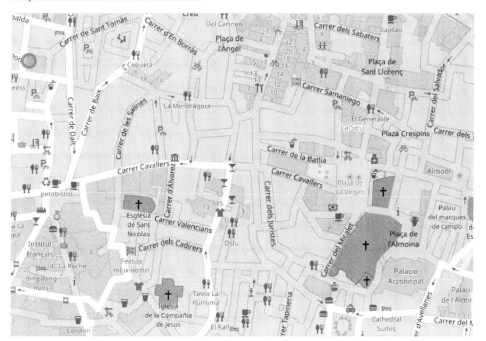

© OpenStreetMap contributors

https://goo.gl/maps/LzgMcmiy72R2

Palau Pineda Café
961 36 20 36 Plaza Carmen 4 Weekdays 14.00 - 17.00

This restaurant is located IN the Palau Pineda, which is now a government building with expositions of paintings. It is opposite of the church, you will see a blackboard outside. Because it is government building I guess, the menu is in Valencian. The inside garden is the terrace, and it is a great place to sit, with shadow from the trees. The **menu del dia** is always delicious, and simple, and a bit imaginative with a nice presentation. At 8, 90 bread wine drink coffee AND desert included., it is one of my favourites.

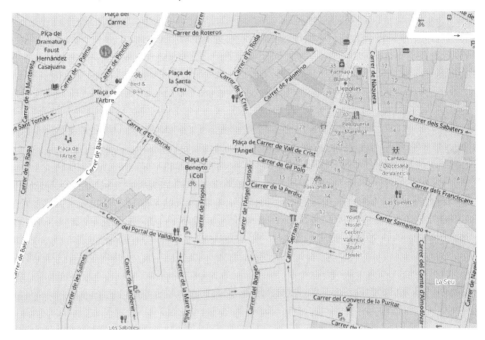

© OpenStreetMap contributors

https://goo.gl/maps/fgqjgPfZpoD2

35

Piko's
Calle Quart, 69 Daily 08.00-00.00

To be honest, I didn't want to share this with the world. It is an absolute no frills place, on a fairly busy road, just outside the old city, near the Torres de Quart. A few tables outside, all Spanish, all noisy. But the food, (there is a **menu del dia**, and loads of fresh tapas), is good and fresh, and cheap. Service is Spanish no nonsense, and no one speaks English. This is not a place to have a nice sit down, but a place to eat simple Spanish tapas.

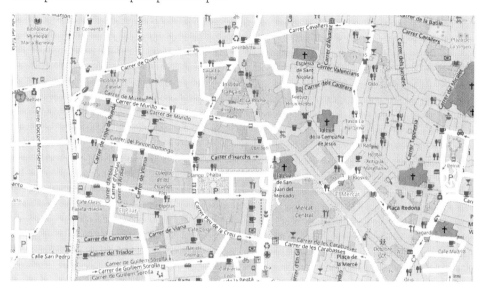

© OpenStreetMap contributors

https://goo.gl/maps/7k8cuhuBSuS2

Taberna El Olivo

Plaza del Arbol 4 Mo-Thu 16.00- 01.30, Fri-Sunday 12.00-01.30

Not a restaurant, but a tapas bar with one of the best terraces in Valencia on a tiny square, under an ancient olive tree that gives the square its name. The tapas are a bit pricey, but they are worth it, because they are super fresh and all homemade. The grilled filleted sardines are still the best I have ever eaten.

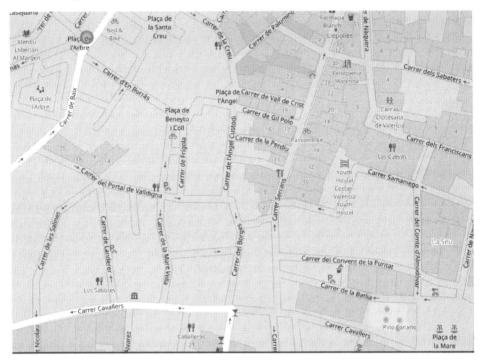

© OpenStreetMap contributors

https://goo.gl/maps/e8MC8bJ4T3T2

Thistinto
960 21 78 14

https://www.facebook.com/Thistinto-759854417419449/

Carrer de Dalt (Calle Alta), 28, Thu-Tue 14.00-16.00 and 20.00- 00.00, Sunday night closed.

A relatively new restaurant, Spanish and Italian mix. A small terrace, and fresh, classic food with a twist, and well prepared too. Very reasonably price menu, 8,95 including wine, and friendly service.

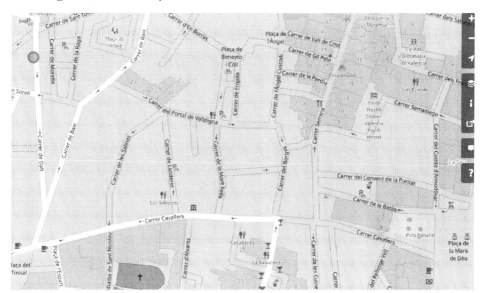

© OpenStreetMap contributors

https://goo.gl/maps/XsWWQo3HJjP2

Food Words Spanish to English

a eligir : to choose from

aceite : olive oil

aceituna (oliva) : olive

agua : water

aguacate : avocado

ajo : garlic

Ajos tiernos : Spring onion

albahaca : basil

albóndiga : meatball

alcachofa : artichoke

alcaparras : capers

almejas : clams

almendras : almonds

almuerzo : lunch

alubias : pulses

alubias negras : black beans

alubias rojas : kidney beans

anchoa : anchovy

arroz : rice

asado : roast

atún : tuna

azafrán : saffron

azúcar : sugar

bacalao : cod

barbacoa : barbecue

bebida : drink

berenjena : aubergine

bocadillo : sandwich

botella : bottle

calabacín : courgette

calabaza : marrow

calamar : squid

caldo : broth

canela : cinnamon

canelones : canneloni

cangrejo : crab

caracol : snail

carne : meat

carne picada : mince

carta : menu

Casera/o : Home made

cebolla : onion

cena : dinner

Centro de mesa : to share

cerdo : pork

cerdo picado : mince pork

cerveza : beer

champiñón : mushroom

cilantro : coriander

ciruela : plum

ciruela (seca) : prune

clara de huevo : egg white

col : cabbage

colar : strain

coles de Bruselas : brussel sprouts

coliflor : cauliflower

combinar : combine

comer : eat

comida : food, meal

comino : cumin

conejo : rabbit

corazones de alcachofa : hearts of artichoke

cordero : lamb

cortado en cuatro : quartered

costillas : ribs

crema : cream

crudo : raw

crujiente : crispy

cuchara : spoon

cuchillo : knife

cuenta : bill, check

dehuesado : boned

desayuno : breakfast

dulce : sweet

en trozos : sliced

Embutidos : Cold cuts of sausages

eneldo : dill

ensalada : salad

entero : whole

Entremeses : Cold cuts of ham and sausages, but it can be a little bit of anything, appetiser

escalfado : poached

escabeche : pickled, cooked with vinegar

espaguetis : spaghetti

espárragos : asparagus

espinacas : spinach

estofado : casserole, stew

exprimido : squeezed

filete : steak

fresa : strawberry

frito : fried

fruta : fruit

galleta : biscuit

gambas : prawns

garbanzos : chick peas

gazpacho : cold tomato soup

guarnición : garnish

guisante : pea

guisada : stewed

habas : broad beans

helado : ice cream

hielo : ice

hierba : herb

hierbabuena : mint

hígado : liver

higo : fig

hinojo : fennel

hoja : leaf

hojaldre : puff pastry

horno : oven

hueso : bone

hueva : roe

huevo : egg

huevo duro : hard boiled egg

bistec : steak

jamón : ham

jamón York : cooked ham

jarra jug : n (f)

jerez : sherry

jugo : juice

jugoso : juicy

lado : side

lata : can

laurel : bayleaf

leche : milk

lechoso : milky

lechuga : lettuce

lentejas : lentils

liebre : hare

lima : lime

limón : lemon

lomo : fillet (tenderloin) but also used for fish

manteca : lard

mantequilla : butter

manzana : apple

marisco : seafood

mayonesa : mayonnaise

mejillones : mussels

melocotón : peach

melón : honeydew melon

membrillo : quince

merluza : hake

mermelada : jam

mesa : table

mezclar : mix

miel : honey

mollejas : sweetbreads

morcilla : black pudding

mostaza : mustard

muslo de pollo : chicken drumstick

naranja : orange

nata : cream

nata agria : sour cream

nata montada : whipped cream

nectarina : nectarine

nuez : nut

nuez (de california) : walnut

nuez moscada : nutmeg

pan : bread

pan de molde : sliced bread

pan integral : brown bread

parrillada : grill

pasa (de uva) : raisin

patata : potato

patatas fritas : french fries

pato : duck

pechuga de pollo : chicken breast

pelado : peeled

pepinillo : gherkin

pepino : cucumber

pera : pear

perejil : parsley

perrito caliente : hot dog

pescado : fish

picante : spicy

pimentón : paprika

pimienta : pepper

pimiento rojo : red pepper

pimiento verde : green pepper

piña : pineapple

piñones : pine kernels

plátano : banana

postre : dessert

propina : tip

puerro : leek

queso : cheese

rabo de buey : oxtail

rallado : grated

rape : monkfish

rebozada : coated, breaded

refresco : soft drink

relleno : filling, stuffing

remolacha : beetroot

reservar : reserve

riñón : kidney

romero : rosemary

sal : salt

salado : salted

salchicha : sausage

salmonete : red mullet

salsa : sauce

salsa de soja : soy sauce

salsa tártara : tartar sauce

saltear : sauté

sed : thirst

segundo plato : main course

seta : mushroom

sidra : cider

sofrito : lightly fried

solomillo : sirloin steak

sopa : soup

tallarines : noodles

tarta de queso : cheesecake

tazón : bowl

té : tea

tenedor : fork

ternera picada : minced beef

tibio : tepid

tierno : tender

tiritas : strips

tomillo : thyme

tortilla de patatas : Spanish omelette

tostada : toast

tostado : toasted

trucha : trout

uva : grape

vapor : steam

verdura : vegetable

vino : Wine (blanco: white; tinto red)

zanahoria : carrot

zapallo : pumpkin

Food Words English to Spanish

almonds : almendras

anchovy : anchoa

apple : manzana

artichoke : alcachofa

asparagus : espárragos

aubergine : berenjena

avocado : aguacate

banana : plátano

barbecue : barbacoa

basil : albahaca

bayleaf : laurel

beer : cerveza

beetroot : remolacha

bill, check : cuenta

biscuit : galleta

black beans : alubias negras

black pudding : morcilla

bone : hueso

boned : dehuesado

bottle : botella

bowl : tazón

bread : pan

breakfast : desayuno

broad beans : habas

broth : caldo

brown bread : pan integral

brussel sprouts : coles de Bruselas

butter : mantequilla

cabbage : col

can : lata

canneloni : canelones

capers : alcaparras

carrot : zanahoria

casserole : estofado

cauliflower : coliflor

cheese : queso

cheesecake : tarta de queso

chick peas : garbanzos

chicken breast : pechuga de pollo

chicken drumstick : muslo de pollo

cider : sidra

cinnamon : canela

clams : almejas

coated, breaded : rebozada

cod : bacalao

Cold cuts : Embutidos, entremeses

cold tomato soup : gazpacho

combine : combinar

cooked ham : jamón York

coriander : cilantro

courgette : calabacín

crab : cangrejo

cream : crema

cream : nata

crispy : crujiente

cucumber : pepino

cumin : comino

dessert : postre

dill : eneldo

dinner : cena

drink : bebida

duck : pato

eat : comer

egg : huevo

egg white : clara de huevo

fennel : hinojo

fig : higo

filling, stuffing : relleno

fish : pescado

food, meal : comida

fork : tenedor

french fries : patatas fritas

fried : frito

fruit : fruta

garlic : ajo

garnish : guarnición

gherkin : pepinillo

grape : uva

grated : rallado

green pepper : pimiento verde

grill : parrillada

hake : merluza

ham : jamón

hard boiled egg : huevo duro

hare : liebre

hearts of artichoke : corazones de alcachofa

herb : hierba

home made ; casera/o

honey : miel

honeydew melon : melón

hot dog : perrito caliente

ice : hielo

ice cream : helado

jam : mermelada

juice : jugo

juicy : jugoso

kidney : riñón

kidney beans : alubias rojas

knife : cuchillo

lamb : cordero

lard : manteca

leaf : hoja

leek : puerro

lemon : limón

lentils : lentejas

lettuce : lechuga

lightly fried : sofrito

lime : lima

liver : hígado

lunch : almuerzo

main course : segundo plato

marrow : calabaza

mayonnaise : mayonesa

meat : carne

meatball : albóndiga

menu : carta

milk : leche

milky : lechoso

mince : carne picada

mince pork : cerdo picado

minced beef : ternera picada

mint : hierbabuena

mix : mezclar

monkfish : rape

mushroom : champiñón

mushroom : seta

mussels : mejillones

mustard : mostaza

n (f) : jarra jug

nectarine : nectarina

noodles : tallarines

nut : nuez

nutmeg : nuez moscada

olive : aceituna (olive)

olive oil : aceite (de olive)

onion : cebolla

orange : naranja

oven : horno

oxtail : rabo de buey

paprika : pimentón

parsley : perejil

pea : guisante

peach : melocotón

pear : pera

peeled : pelado

pepper : pimienta

pine kernels : piñones

pineapple : piña

plum : ciruela

poached : escalfado

pork : cerdo

potato : patata

prawns : gambas

prune : ciruela (seca)

puff pastry : hojaldre

pulses : alubias

pumpkin : zapallo

quartered : cortado en cuatro

quince : membrillo

rabbit : conejo

raisin : pasa (de uva)

raw : crudo

red mullet : salmonete

red pepper : pimiento rojo

reserve : reservar

ribs : costillas

rice : arroz

roast : asado

roe : hueva

rosemary : romero

saffron : azafrán

salad : ensalada

salt : sal

salted : salado

sandwich : bocadillo

sauce : salsa

sausage : salchicha

sauté : saltear

seafood : marisco

Share food : a compartir, centro de mesa

sherry : jerez

side : lado

sirloin steak : solomillo

sliced : en trozos

sliced bread : pan de molde

snail : caracol

soft drink : refresco

soup : sopa

sour cream : nata agria

soy sauce : salsa de soja

spaghetti : espaguetis

spanish omelette : tortilla de patatas

spicy : picante

spinach : espinacas

spoon : cuchara

spring onions : Ajos Tiernos

squeeze : exprimir

squid : calamar

steak : filete

steak : bistec

steam : vapour

stewed : guisado

strain : colar

strawberry : fresa

strips : tiritas

sugar : azúcar

sweet : dulce

sweetbreads : mollejas

table : mesa

tartar sauce : salsa tártara

tea : té

tender : tierno

tepid : tibio

thirst : sed

thyme : tomillo

tip : propina

to choose from : a elegir

toast : tostada

toasted : tostado

trout : trucha

tuna : atún

vegetable : verdura

walnut : nuez (de california)

water : agua

whipped cream : nata montada

wine : vino (white: blanco; red: tinto)

whole : entero

Printed in Great Britain
by Amazon